How to get

... by a cat

Written and Illustrated

by

Lynda Sellers

Order this book online at www.trafford.com
or email orders@trafford.com

Most Trafford titles are also available at major online book retailers.

© Copyright 2011, 2012 Lynda Sellers.

All rights reserved. No part of this publication may be reproduced, stored in a retrieval system, or transmitted, in any form or by any means, electronic, mechanical, photocopying, recording, or otherwise, without the written prior permission of the author.

Printed in the United States of America.

ISBN: 978-1-4269-8876-9

Library of Congress Control Number: 2011913940

Trafford rev. 01/26/2012

North America & international
toll-free: 1 888 232 4444 (USA & Canada)
phone: 250 383 6864 ♦ fax: 812 355 4082

"Let's have a wee chat";
said the pup to the cat,

"for I truly must know how it is that one gets

"...by a cat"

"Oh, p...l...e...a...s...e!!!!!!!!

you cannot mean that you haven't a clue", quizzed the cat to the pup with a hint of a **SMIRK**

.......for he'd already **dished out** quite a few

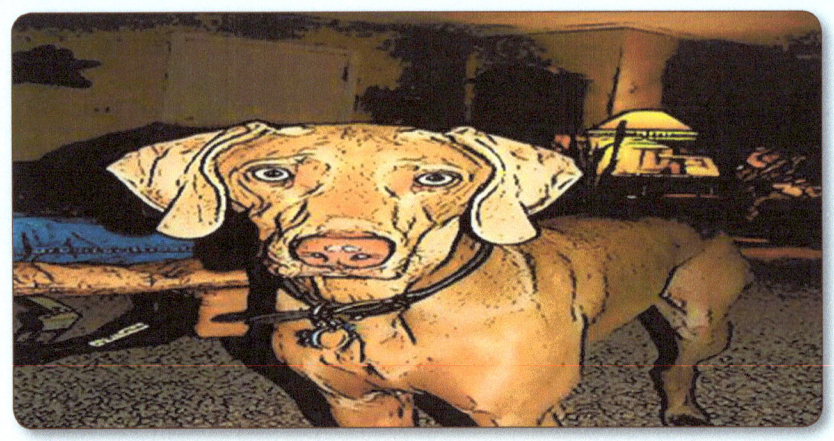

"Oh I know what it is to get

...by a cat

"but what I simply don't get;

is the **how** or the

why ?????

of the

WHACK

...by a cat."

"And pray tell why do you care?",

groaned the cat to the pup

in utter

despair.

"For if you are

by a cat

"the how and the why matter little

by the fact of the

WHACK."

"Oh but it is; don't you see,"...

...or it is so for

"for I wish never to be

WHACKED

in the least little bit...

like he".

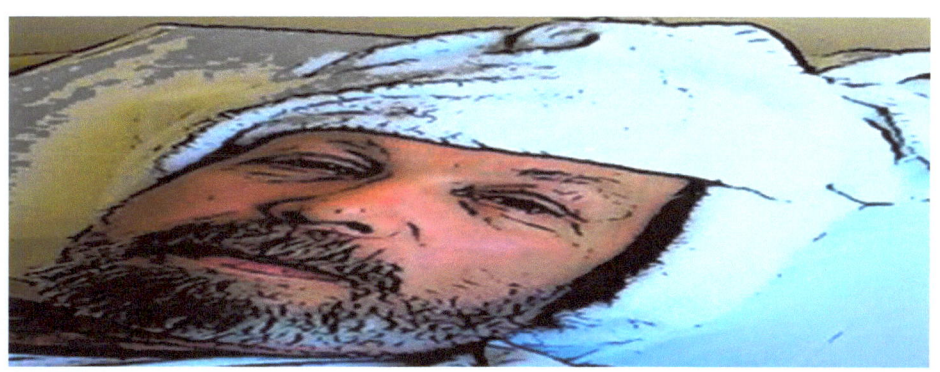

With a turn of his head,

the cat laughed a purr

as he saw the man

 ;

 as a matter of fact,

had truly and rudely been

...by a cat.

"I see" **sighed**

the cat without a hint of a care;

and then turning aside

he dismissed the pup,

as he swished his tail in the air.

But the pup was not done!

To the pup; their wee chat had just begun!

So with little or no thought

she did

precisely what

ought

not!

and jumped over the cats

back...

And directly in reach of a

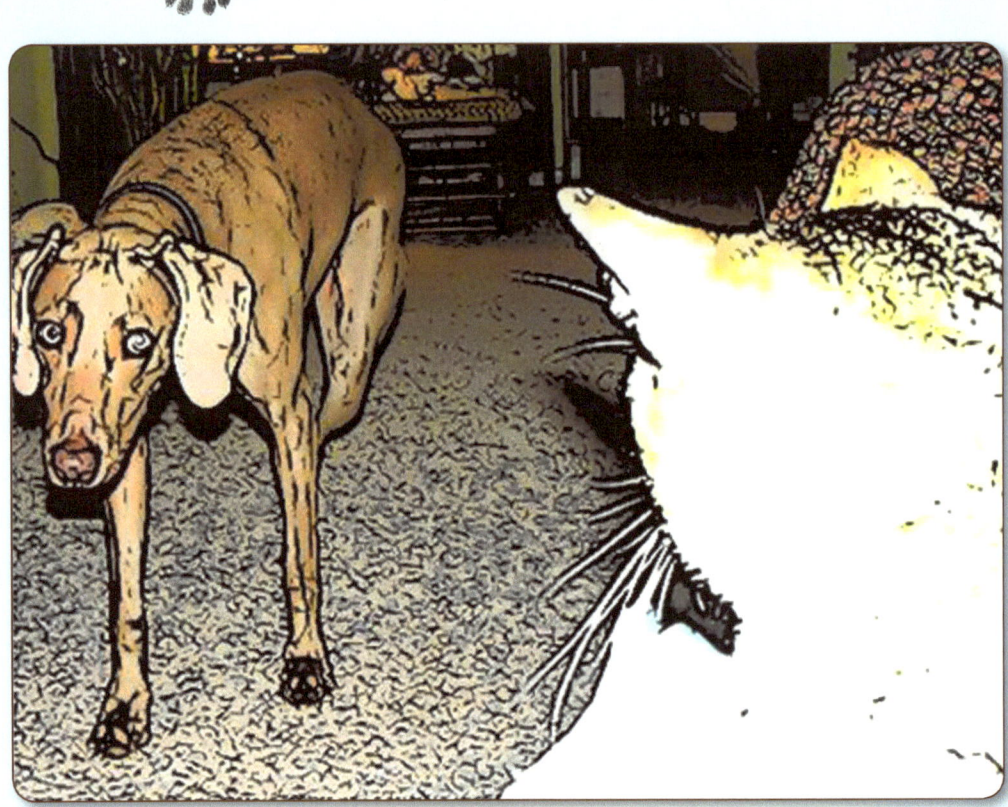

...by a cat ...

"I see you are not the

brightest

of pups."

said the

cat,

as he delivered the

WHACK,

"for that is a most excellent

to get

...by a cat.

Later that day, the pup could not stay away as she spied the cat with one of her toys.

To the pup this meant

and thus came another

...for the day.

For the rest of the
day the cat thought
the pup understood,

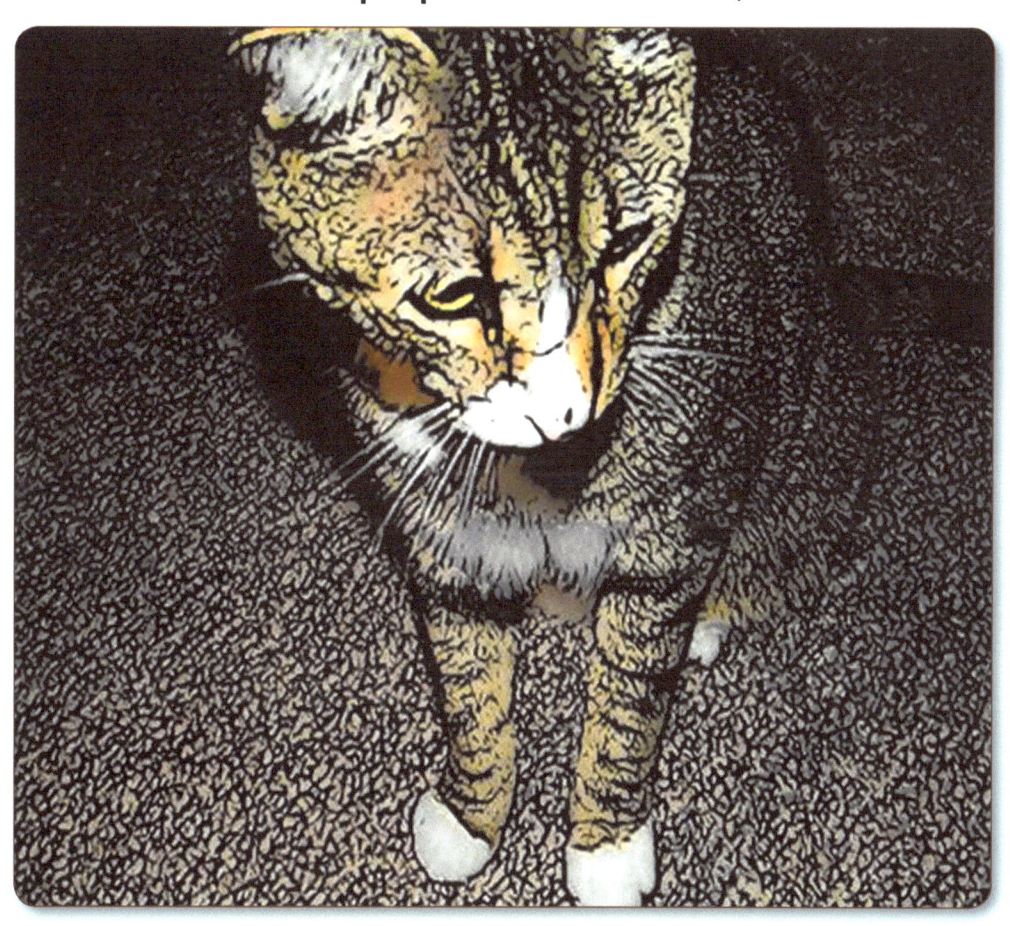

he delivered the whacks for the pups

own good!!!

And thus did it go;

for the pup

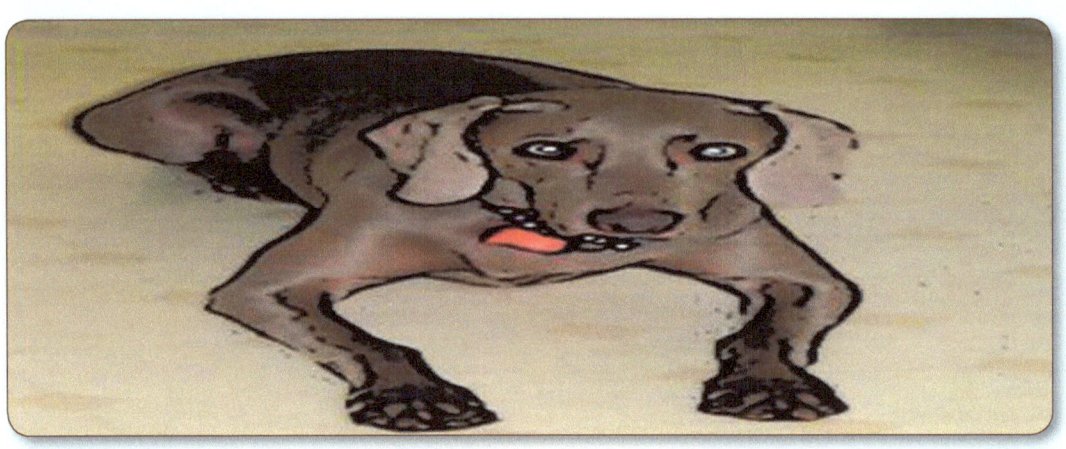

and the cat,.....

as the pup received

after

after

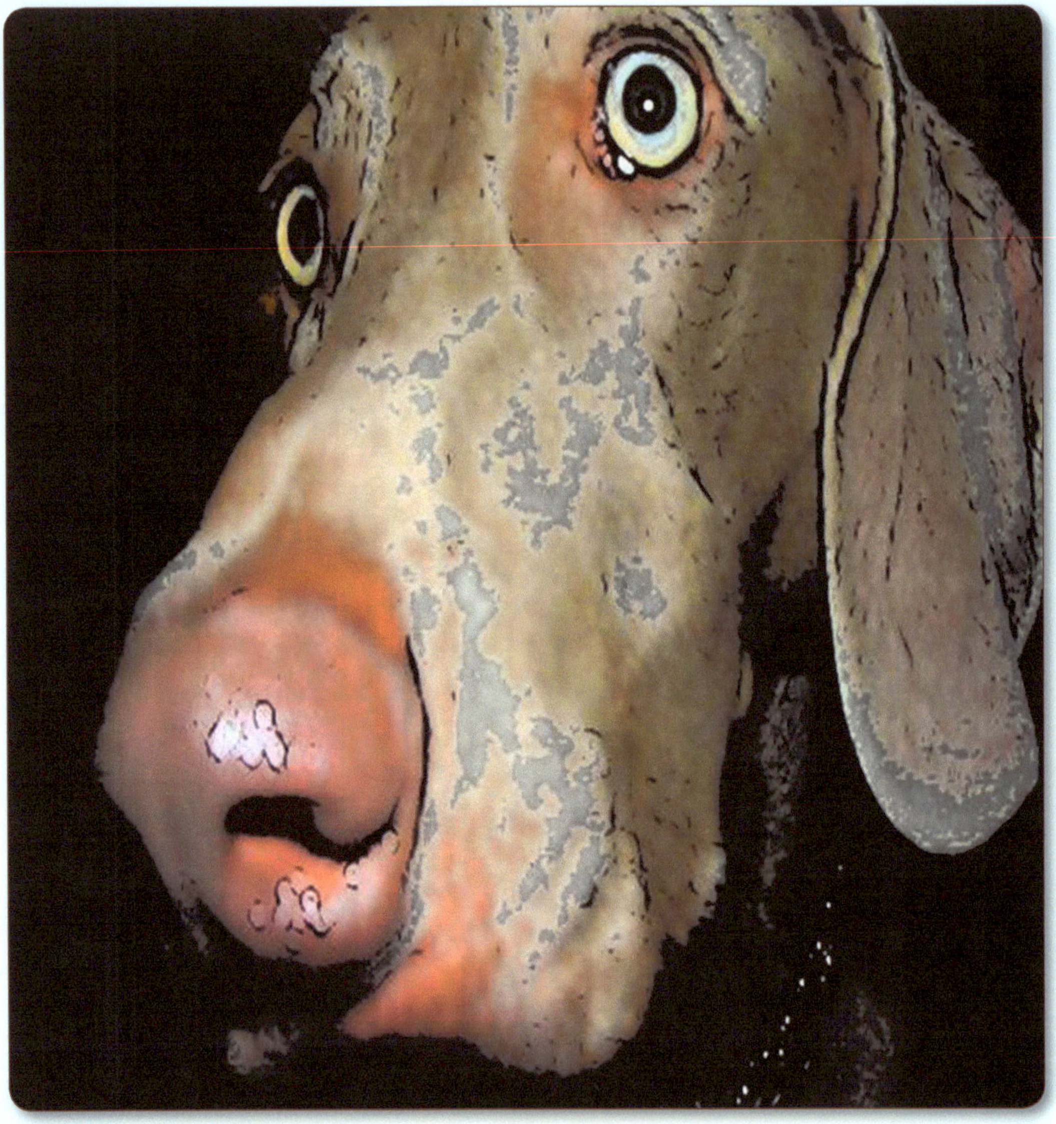

The pup learned that barking to bark;

as pups often do

is one **SUREFIRE** way to get a

WHACK

thumped

on you.

Taking a snooze;

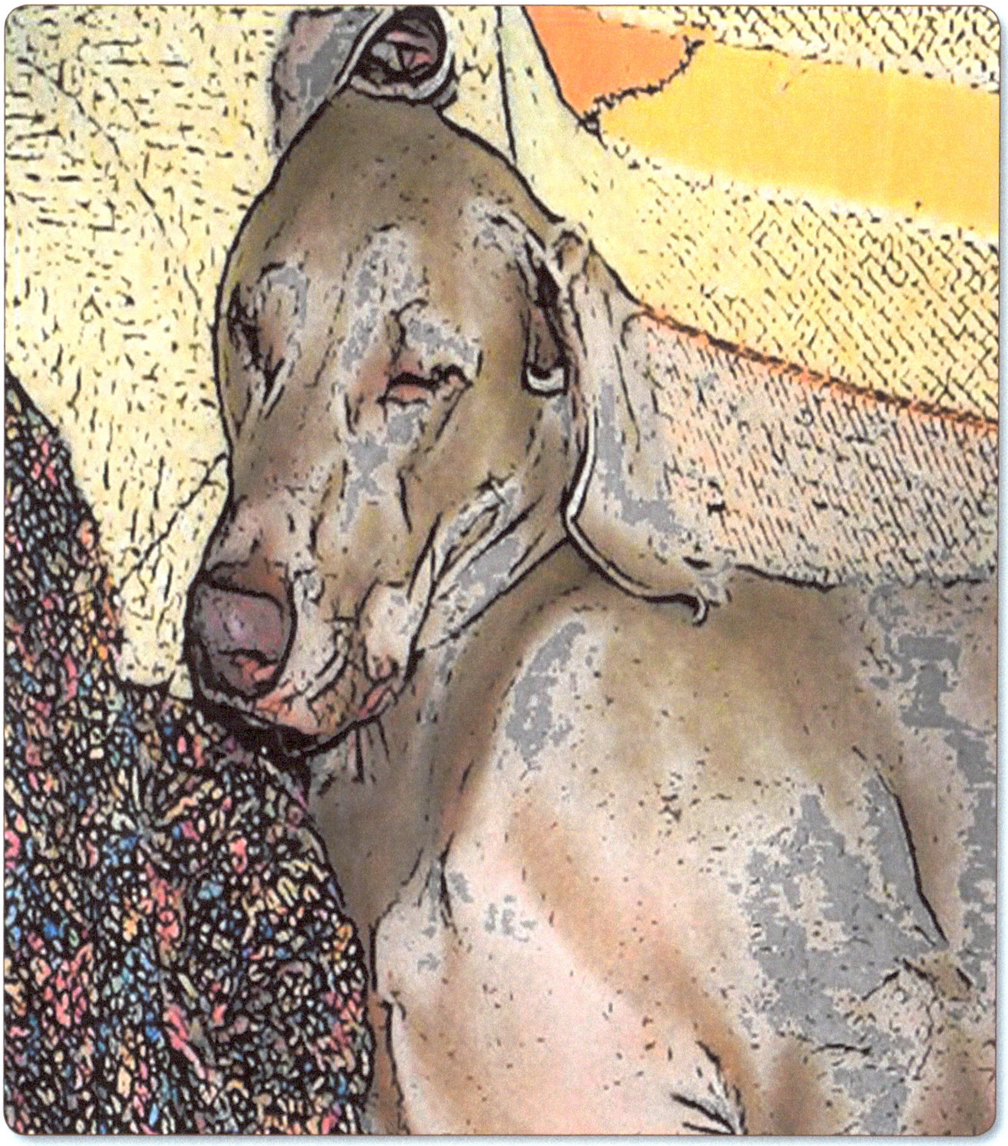

Or acting the fool

Will more often than *not*;

earn you a

WHACK

or two.

She learned some whacks are given with no rhyme or reason;

And more times than 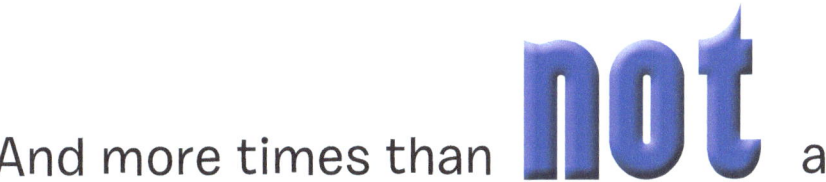 a

hurts like a whack from a

pretty big kitten.

But the

long

and the

short

of the

"...by a cat."

is what you choose to accept

when you get yourself

You can get all

and throw one

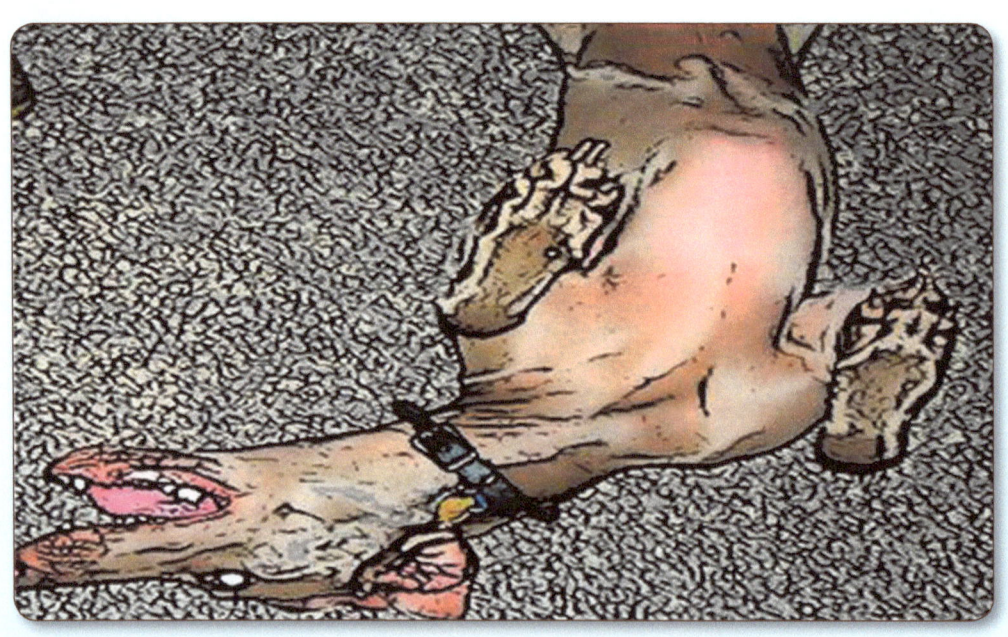

Or mutter to yourself; saying,

"I don't like this,"........

........"No; not one little bit."

You can pray;

You can pout;

You can sing ♫ ♪ ♫

 or you can shout!

But only God can help you figure it out.

For into each life a  will come...

And for **MOST** of us, there

are **MORE**

than **one,**

But it is

in the

 or the

 or

even the

What matters the most is

HOW you **HANDLE** the

WHACK

"The End"

God tells us in James 1:2 to "Consider it all joy, my brethren, when you encounter various trials, knowing that the testing of your faith produces endurance."

This book is lovingly dedicated to my husband, Dwight, who was truly and rudely ... **WHACKED** when he was diagnosed with Parkinson's disease in 2006 and then whacked again on February 28, 2007 when he underwent surgery for a brain tumor.

His faith, courage and humor have been shining examples of how God's grace will carry you through the whacks of life.

www.ingramcontent.com/pod-product-compliance
Lightning Source LLC
Chambersburg PA
CBHW040057160426
43192CB00002B/93